The
# SIDEWAYS
Guide to Wine and Life

# The SIDEWAYS
## Guide to Wine and Life

Screenplay by
**Alexander Payne** & **Jim Taylor**

Based on the Novel by
**Rex Pickett**

Photography by
**Merie W. Wallace**

Illustrations by
**Robert Neubecker**

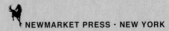

NEWMARKET PRESS · NEW YORK

Screenplay extracts, photographs and artwork © 2004 Twentieth Century
Fox Film Corporation. All rights reserved.
Extracts on pages 38-39 from the novel *Sideways* by Rex Pickett
© 2004 Rex Pickett. Used by permission of St. Martin's Press.

Maps on pages 13, 15, 16, 19 by Bob Dickey courtesy of
Santa Barbara Conference & Visitors Bureau and Film Commission.
www.santabarbaraCA.com

This book may not be reproduced, in whole or in part, in any form,
without written permission. Inquiries should be addressed to:
Permissions Department, Newmarket Press,
18 East 48th Street, New York, NY 10017.

This book is published in the United States of America.

ISBN 978-1-55704-686-4

Also available from Newmarket Press
***Sideways: The Shooting Script***
Screenplay by Alexander Payne and Jim Taylor, Based on the novel by
Rex Pickett, Introduction by Peter Travers, Afterword by Rex Pickett
(ISBN 978-1-55704-655-0)

QUANTITY PURCHASES
Companies, professional groups, clubs, and other organizations may qualify
for special terms when ordering quantities of this title. For information,
write to Special Sales, Newmarket Press, 18 East 48th Street, New York,
NY 10017; call (212) 832-3575 or 1-800-669-3903; FAX (212) 832-3629;
or e-mail info@newmarketpress.com.

**www.newmarketpress.com**

Produced by Newmarket Productions: Esther Margolis, director;
Frank DeMaio production manager; Keith Hollaman, managing editor.

Edited by Linda Sunshine.

Designed by Timothy Shaner, Night & Day Design.

10  9  8  7  6  5  4  3

**M**ost of us are prepared, more or less, for the ups and downs of life. But it is the sideways journeys that make us lose our way.

And the two most lost people in the house are Miles (Paul Giamatti) and Jack (Thomas Haden Church).

Who are these guys? Miles is an un-recovered divorcé and would-be novelist with a wine fixation. Jack, his college buddy, is a washed-up actor about to settle for marriage, a job with his future father-in-law, and life in the suburbs.

A week before Jack's wedding, Miles decides they should take a celebratory trip to the vineyards of the Santa Ynez Valley. Thus begins their misadventures and a truly inebriated, sideways-skewed road trip.

The two couldn't be an odder couple. Jack is an over-sexed charmer; Miles is a sad-sack worrier. Jack is fine with cheap Merlot; Miles pines for the elusive, perfect Pinot. On vacation, Miles only wants to drink some good wine, play golf, eat great food, and enjoy the scenery. Jack wants to get laid.

Not surprisingly, Jack makes an instant love connection with Stephanie (Sandra Oh) while Miles feebly stumbles towards romance with Maya

(Virginia Madsen), tripping over his own feet every step of the way.

During their week of mad lust and outright betrayals the boys will encounter barrels of wine, a lot of gorgeous scenery, and a very angry, big fat, naked guy.

Running through the comedy and mixed emotions of the movie is a constant stream of wine — red wine, white wine, cheap wine, precious wine, wine that brings friends closer, wine that's abused and, of course, wine that seals a kiss. Wine is, in fact, a principal player in this movie, as well as a metaphor for the lives of the characters who play out the angst and muddle of modern life.

This little book is a celebration of the movie, the novel upon which it is based, and the beauty and splendor of wine country. Here are life lessons and wine recommendations, places to visit in the Santa Ynez Valley that were featured in the movie, tips for tasting wine, and a few truly great bottles of wine. Enjoy. And remember, D-and-D (drinking and dialing) can be dangerous to your love life.

Life Uncorked

# Touring the
# Santa Ynez
# Valley

# with
# Two Guys
# Tasting Wine

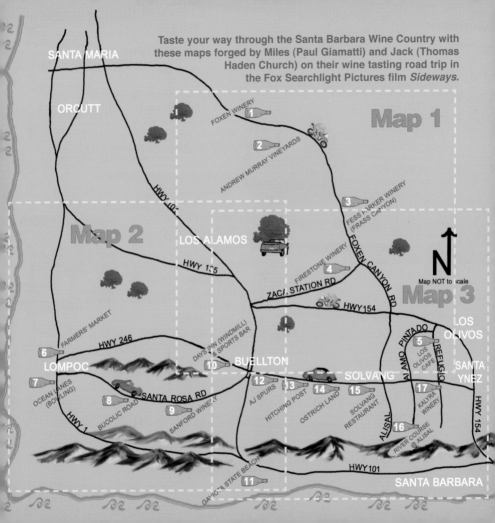

# Map 1 Listings

## 1 FOXEN WINERY

7200 Foxen Canyon Road
Santa Maria
805.937.4251
www.santamaria.com

*During the split
screen portion of the
film, Miles and Jack
help themselves to full
glasses when the pourer turns her back.*

## 2 ANDREW MURRAY VINEYARDS

(Tasting Room: 2901-A Grand Avenue)
Los Olivos
805.686.9604
www.andrewmurrayvineyards.com

*Some of the most bucolic images in the
movie come as Miles and Jack drive
through these vineyards.*

## 3 FESS PARKER WINERY (FRASS CANYON)

6200 Foxen Canyon Road
Los Olivos
805.688.1545
www.fessparker.com
10am-5pm daily

*At "Frass Canyon's" large wine tasting
event, Miles phones his agent and finds
out his book will not be published.
After the pourer refuses to serve him a
full glass, Miles guzzles the spit bucket.*

## 4 FIRESTONE WINERY

5000 Zaca Station Road, Los Olivos
805.688.3940
www.firestonewine.com
10am-5pm daily

*Miles, Jack, Maya and
Stephanie sneak out of a
wine lecture to share a
romantic walk through
the Barrel Room.*

## 5 LOS OLIVOS CAFE & WINE MERCHANT

2879 Grand Avenue, Los Olivos
888.946.3748
www.losolivoscafe.com

*Miles, Jack, Maya and
Stephanie enjoy dinner
and several exquisite
bottles of wine.*

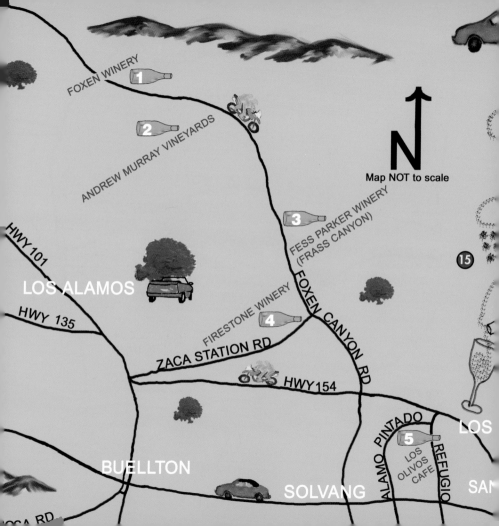

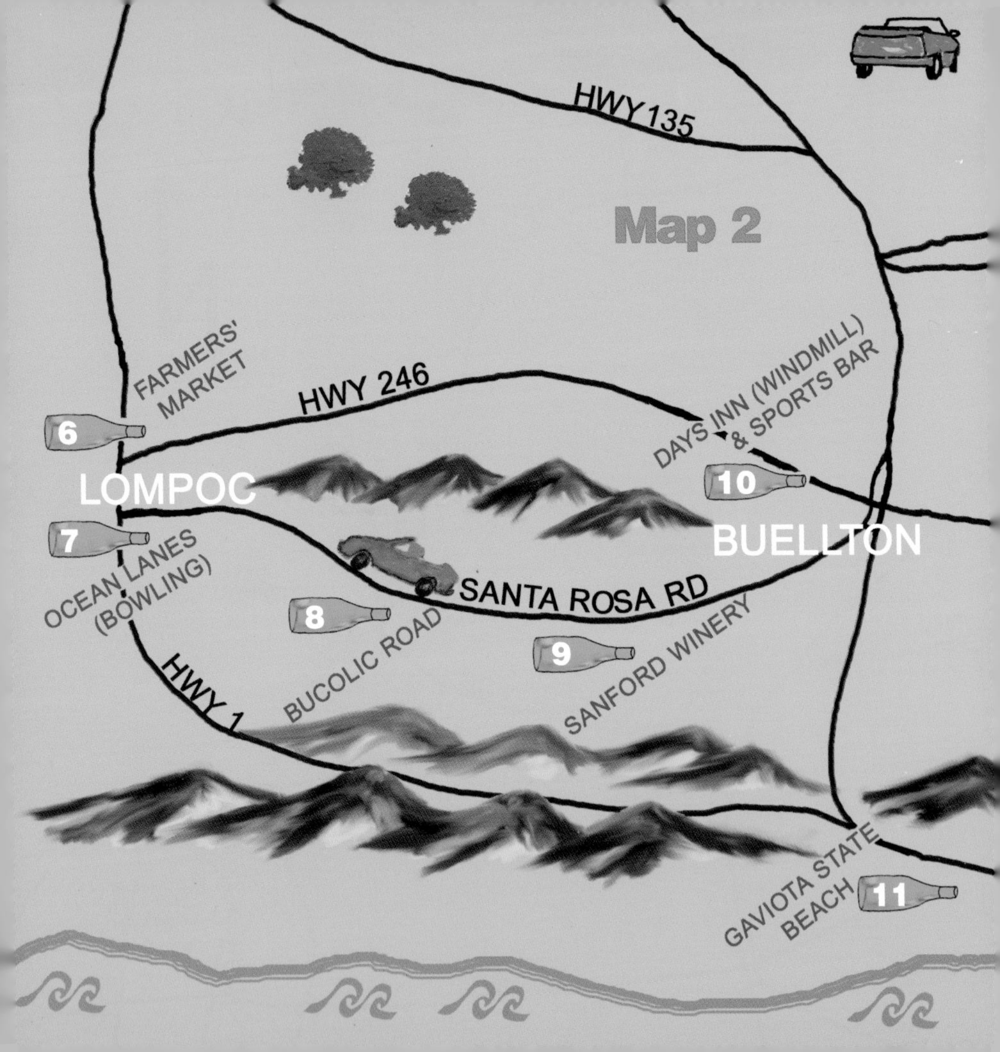

HWY 135

Map 2

FARMERS' MARKET

HWY 246

6

DAYS INN (WINDMILL) & SPORTS BAR

LOMPOC

10

7

BUELLTON

OCEAN LANES (BOWLING)

SANTA ROSA RD

8

BUCOLIC ROAD

9

SANFORD WINERY

HWY 1

GAVIOTA STATE BEACH

11

# Map 2 Listings

## **6** LOMPOC FARMERS' MARKET

Corner of Ocean Avenue & "I", Lompoc
805.459.6050
www.lompoc.com
2pm–6pm Fridays

*Miles and Maya walk through the market.*

## **7** OCEAN LANES

1420 E. Ocean Avenue, Lompoc
www.lompoc.com
805.736.4541

*Miles begrudgingly joins Jack at the bowling alley with Stephanie, her daughter and talkative mother.*

## **8** BUCOLIC SANTA ROSA ROAD

Between Highway 1 and Highway 101
South of Highway 246

*Jack and Miles drive through vineyards and rolling hills.*

## **9** SANFORD WINERY

7250 Santa Rosa Road, Buellton
805.688.3300
www.sanfordwinery.com

*Miles teaches Jack the basics of wine tasting. Chris Burroughs starts them off with the Vin Gris in which Miles smells citrus, strawberry, the faintest soupçon of asparagus and just a flutter of a nutty edam cheese.*

## **10** DAYS INN & CLUB-HOUSE SPORTS BAR

114 E. Highway 246, Buellton
805.688.8448
www.daysinn-solvang.com

*The motel Miles and Jack stay in while in Buellton.*

## **11** GAVIOTA STATE BEACH

Highway 101
33 miles west of Santa Barbara
805.968.1033
www.parks.ca.gov

*Jack consoles Miles after his publisher rejects his novel.*

# Map 3 Listings

**12** **AJ SPURS**
350 E. Highway 246, Buellton
805.686.1655
www.ajspurs.com

*Miles and Jack meet Cami, Jack's calamitous one-night stand.*

**13** **HITCHING POST II**
406 E. Highway 246, Buellton
805.688.0676
www.hitchingpostwines.com

*Miles and Jack share a bottle of Highliner at the bar. While having dinner, they talk to Maya who waits tables there. Later, Miles returns on his own.*

**14** **OSTRICH LAND**
610 E. Highway 246
(between Buellton and Solvang)
805.686.9696
www.ostrichland.com

*Ostriches seen while Miles, Jack, Maya and Stephanie drive to the picnic. Later, Jack gets acquainted with them on his "run" from Buellton to Solvang.*

**15** **SOLVANG RESTAURANT**
1672 Copenhagen Drive, Solvang
805.688.4645
www.solvangrestaurant.com

*As they sit down for breakfast, Jack grumpily insists that Miles' gloominess not thwart his attempts to get lucky before the wedding.*

**16** **RIVER COURSE AT THE ALISAL GUEST RANCH**
150 Alisal Road, Solvang
805.688.6042
www.rivercourse.com

*While golfing, Miles and Jack frighten the impatient foursome hitting into them.*

**17** **KALYRA WINERY**
343 N. Refugio Road, Santa Ynez
805.693.8864
www.kalyrawinery.com

*While tasting wine, Miles and Jack meet Stephanie, a flirtatious wine pourer who becomes the object of Jack's affection.*

18

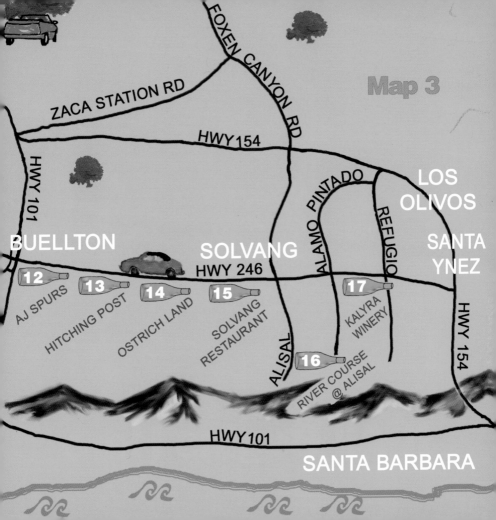

# Tips for Touring Wine Country

**Miles:** We head north, begin the grape tour up there, making our way south so the more we drink the closer we get to the motel.

# Transverse Valleys

*The boys now pass vineyards of immaculate grapevines.*

**MILES**
Jesus, *what a day!* Isn't it gorgeous? And the ocean's just right over that ridge. See, the reason this region's great for Pinot is that the cold air off the Pacific flows in at night through these transverse valleys and cools down the berries. Pinot's a very thin-skinned grape and doesn't like heat or humidity.

# Sideways Wine List

**T**he wines featured in the movie include:

Byron 1992 Sparkling
Sanford Vin Gris
Kalyra Chardonnay
Kalyra Cab Franc
Fiddle Head Sauvignon Blanc
Whitcraft 2001 Pinot Noir
Sea Smoke Botella Pinot Noir
Kistler Sonoma Coast Pinot Noir
Latour Pommard 1er Cru
Hitching Post Bien Nacido Pinot Noir
Hitching Post Highliner Pinot Noir
Andrew Murray Syrah
'61 Cheval Blanc

# Wine Tastin

## 11:00 - 4:0

g Hours

0 daily

29

# Wine Tasting 101

**MILES**
First take your glass and examine the wine against the light.  You're looking at color and clarity.

**JACK**
What color is it supposed to be?

**MILES**
Depends on the varietal. Just get a sense of it. Thick? Thin? Watery? Syrupy? Inky? Amber, whatever.

**JACK**
Huh.

**MILES**
Now tip it. What you're doing here is checking for color density as it thins toward the rim. Tells you how old it is, among other things, usually more important with reds. This is a very young wine, so it's going to retain its color pretty solidly. Now stick your nose in it. Don't be shy. Get your nose in there.What do you smell?

**JACK**
I don't know. Wine? Fermented grapes?

**Miles and Jack checking their wine samples against the light in the Sanford Winery Tasting Room.**

**MILES**
There's not much there yet, but you can still find... a little citrus... maybe some strawberry... passion fruit... and there's even a hint of like asparagus... or like a nutty Edam cheese.

**JACK**
Huh. Maybe a little strawberry. Yeah, strawberry. I'm not so sure about the cheese.

**MILES**
Now set your glass down and get some air into it. Oxygenating it opens it up, unlocks the aroma and the flavors. Very important. Now we smell again.

**JACK**
When do we get to drink it?

**MILES**
Now.

**JACK**
So how would you rate this one?

**MILES**
Usually they start you on the wines with learning disabilities, but this one's pretty damn good.

**JACK** (to Miles)
You know, you could work in a wine store.

**MILES**
Are you chewing gum?

# Good Wood

INT. FOXEN WINERY – DAY
*Miles has just downed a taste of red wine.*

**MILES**
How much skin and stem contact?

**POURER**
About four weeks.

**MILES**
That explains all the tannins. And how long in oak?

**POURER**
About a year.

**MILES**
French or American?

**POURER**
Both.

**MILES**
Good stuff.

**JACK**
Yeah, oak. That's a good wood.

# Jack Catches On

**JACK**
Stephanie took me out into the Pinot fields today. It was awesome. I think I finally got a handle on the whole process, from the soil to the vine to the — what do you call it? — selection and harvest. And the whole, you know, big containers where they mix it. We even ate Pinot grapes right off the vine. Still a little sour but already showing potential for great structure.

Yesterday he didn't know Pinot Noir from Film Noir.

**Merlot** is an easy-drinking red wine that has become extremely popular in the U.S. **Says Miles:** *Merlot, a quintessential grape, when left to its own devices almost always—Pétrus notwithstanding—results in a bland, characterless wine.*

**Chardonnay** is a popular fruit-forward white. **Says Miles:** *Chardonnay is the most corrupted varietal in the world.*

**Pinot** is considered the premiere red wine grape and is known for its complex, difficult-to-perfect flavors. **Says Miles:** *Pinot is a finicky, elusive, but rewarding varietal.*

**Champagne,** the most famous sparkling wine, is named for its region of origin in France. A process of double fermentation makes the tiny bubbles. **Says Miles:** *Champagne is a perfect transition between more serious wines, perfect when I didn't want to sober up but didn't want to goose-step into the void either.*

# What Are We Drinking, Miles?

**Syrah** is a dark, full-bodied, strong red wine that is best appreciated when served with food. **Says Miles:** *We had abandoned the subtlety of Pinot for the pure unadulterated lust of Syrah.*

**Cabernet** is a red wine famed for its rich, fruity flavors and heavy tannins. **Says Miles:** *Cabs can be rich and powerful and exalting, but they usually seem prosaic to me for some reason.*

**Riesling** is a sweeter white wine often served with dessert, though gaining in popularity as a dinner wine. **Says Miles:** *I used to think Riesling was indicative of an unsophisticated palate, lack of taste, but not anymore.*

**Sauvignon Blanc** is a lighter white wine featuring herbal flavors; it is considered the new alternative to Chardonnay. **Says Miles:** *The Sauvignon was steely: mineral and gunmetal on the palate, but bright and citrusy.*

—All quotes by Miles from the novel

# Eating & Drinking

*C*hoosing the right wine to match your meal is not as easy as red with red meat, white with fish and foul. Take this handy-dandy guide to make sure you always have the correct wine to match your meal or your mood.

| FLAVORS | Delicate | Hearty, Earthy | Spicy, Pungent |
|---|---|---|---|
| WINE TYPE | Sauvignon Blanc, Riesling Chardonnay | Sangiovese, Pinot Noir, Merlot | Zinfandel, Cabernet Sauvignon, Syrah |
| LOCATION | Starbucks | Her apartment | Motel Six |
| FOODS | Lean Cuisine | Kentucky Fried Chicken | McDonald's |
| HERBS | Salt | Pepper | Ketchup |
| CHEESE | Goat or other smelly ones | American, Cheese Whiz® | Any type of pizza topping |
| PREPARATION | Microwaved, Reheated | Delivery, Take-Out | Not yet defrosted |

# More Tips for Wine Drinking

Keep a record of the wines that you like. It is a mistake to rely on your memory, as anyone who drinks a lot of wine will tell you.

Drink one glass of water for every glass of wine and remember to sit near a rest room.

Drink young wines before old wines and serve the expensive wine before switching to the cheaper one. If you pour the cheap wine into the empty bottles of the more expensive one, your guests may never know the difference.

Wine is best enjoyed when first opened. White wines will last for 2 days if re-corked and refrigerated; red for three or four days but, of course, the best course of action is to finish off all half-emptied bottles once your guests have departed.

Wines, like people, like to breathe so open your bottle about 30 minutes before serving, if you can wait that long.

A colorless glass will show off a wine's color and the ideal vessel has a bulbous base and inwardly sloping sides. In a pinch, though, a Dixie cup will also work but it is never considered good manners to drink straight from the bottle.

Store wine in your underground wine cellar in a custom-made wine rack at an optimum temperature of 52°F (11°C). If you do not have an underground cellar in your apartment, then wine can be stored on top of your refrigerator.

When tasting wine, do not chew gum.

# Vacations Can Be Dangerous

# Days of Wine & Neurosis

**JACK**
You still seeing that shrink?

**MILES**
I went on Monday. But I spent most of the time helping him with his computer.

# No Going to the Dark Side

**JACK**
Please just try to be your normal humorous self, okay? Like who you were before the tailspin. Do you remember that guy? People love that guy. And don't forget your novel is coming out in the fall.

**MILES**
Oh yeah? How exciting. What's it called?

**JACK**
Do not sabotage me. If you want to be a lightweight, that's your call. But do not sabotage me.

**MILES**
Aye-aye, captain.

**JACK**
If they want to drink Merlot, we're drinking Merlot!

**MILES**
If anyone orders Merlot, I'm leaving. I am not drinking any fucking Merlot!

**JACK**
Okay, okay. Relax Miles, Jesus. No Merlot. Did you bring your Xanax?

*Miles takes a SMALL BOTTLE from his pocket and rattles it.*

**JACK** (cont'd)
And don't drink too much. I don't want you going to the dark side or passing out. Do you hear me? No going to the dark side.

# D-and-D

**MILES**
I'm fine!

*But in throwing open his arms for emphasis, he spills a WATER GLASS. Jack rights it and throws a napkin on the tablecloth.*

50

**JACK**
Where were you?

**MILES**
Bathroom.

**JACK**
Did you drink and dial?

*Miles's silence confirms his guilt and shame.*

**JACK** (cont'd)
Why do you always do this? Victoria's gone, man. Gone. Poof.

*Miles looks down and squeezes his eyes tight while pushing out an exhale through his nose.*

# A Wine for Every Occasion

It is always important to match the wine to the occasion. Serving champagne at a funeral, for instance, is considered extremely bad taste, especially if you stand to inherit the family fortune from the deceased. Here are some guidelines:

**First Date:** Serve a young wine or a wine spritzer so that your date does not think you are a wino.

**Second Date:** Go for it! A nice Pinot Noir or Syrah will impress your date and may get you to the third date.

**Dinner with her Parents:** Bring a bottle of very expensive wine if you want to impress your future in-laws. Leave the price tag on the wine and then act surprised when your host or hostess notices how much you have spent. Pretend you are annoyed with the clerk at the wine shop.

**Gym:** White wines are appropriate for cardio work, red for weight training and a light Bordeaux is perfect for Pilates or Yoga. If you have a personal trainer, remember to bring along an extra wine glass.

**Dining Out:** Review the wine list carefully. Select a California wine so that you do not have to pretend to speak French or Italian.

**Drinks with a Married Man:** For this, or any other impending inappropriate relationships, the rule of thumb is that quantity, not quality, is what matters. Keep your budget in mind as you will probably consume several bottles.

**Breaking Up:** See above.

# Wine Is the Occasion

**MAYA**
So what gems do you have in your collection?

**MILES**
Not much of a collection really. I haven't had the wallet for that, so I sort of live bottle to bottle. But I've got a couple things I'm saving. I guess the star would be a 1961 Cheval Blanc.

**MAYA**
You've got a '61 Cheval Blanc that's just sitting there? Go get it. Right now. Hurry up...

*Miles laughs, fights back a bit.*

**MAYA** (cont'd)
Seriously, the '61s are peaking, aren't they? At least that's what I've read. It might be too late already. What are you waiting for?

**MILES**
I don't know. Special occasion. With the right person. It was supposed to be for my tenth wedding anniversary.

**MAYA**
The day you open a '61 Cheval Blanc, that's the special occasion.

Jack
Thomas Haden Church

Miles
Paul Giamatti

56

Maya
Virginia Madsen

Stephanie
Sandra Oh

# Mix and Match

*ines, like people, have distinctive characteristics. Each of the following wines describes one of the characters in* Sideways. *Can you match the wine to the character?*

**A** **Sauvignon Blanc**
Very fresh and designed to be consumed young as age tends to bring out the weaker aspects of the grape. Has an intense taste and aroma that is easy to recognize. Sauvignon Blanc is zestier than other bland wines and likes to mix with other grapes, likes that a lot.

**B** **White Bordeaux**
Dry and witty, these wines are fabulous when young but improve greatly with age, becoming sweeter, more intense and delightfully more full-bodied.

**C** **Pinot Noir**
Extremely sensitive, difficult and expensive to produce or understand. Rarely blended with other grapes, Pinot Noir needs a lot of work, patience and attention but, under the right conditions, can be very stimulating.

**D** **Syrah**
Dark, strong and fairly tannic when young but, if kept for more than three years, Syrah can be very rewarding. These wines are easily adaptable, thrive in warm places and are best enjoyed with food, friends and extra condoms.

Answers on page 64.

**Pinot** is a hard grape to grow. As you know. It's thin-skinned, temperamental, ripens early. It's not a survivor like Cabernet that can grow anywhere and thrive when neglected. Pinot needs constant care and attention and in fact can only grow in specific little tucked-away corners of the world. And only the most patient and nurturing

# Miles Is a Pinot Boy

growers can do it really, can tap into Pinot's most fragile, delicate qualities. Only when someone has taken the time to truly understand its potential can Pinot be coaxed into its fullest expression. And when that happens, its flavors are the most haunting and brilliant and subtle and thrilling and ancient on the planet.

—Miles, from the screenplay

# A Girl's POV:
## Maya on Wine

**I do** like to think about the life of wine, how it's a living thing. I like to think about what was going on the year the grapes were growing, how the sun was shining that summer or if it rained… what the weather was like. I think about all those people who tended and picked the grapes, and if it's an old wine, how many of them must be dead by now. I love how wine continues to evolve, how every

time I open a bottle it's going to taste different than if I had opened it any other day. Because a bottle of wine is actually alive — it's constantly evolving and gaining complexity. That is, until it peaks — like your '61 — and begins its steady, inevitable decline. And it tastes so fucking good.

—From the screenplay

# A Conundrum

Why does Miles criticize Cabernet Franc when in fact the special wine he's been saving for years—a 1961 Cheval Blanc—is made almost entirely from Cabernet Franc? What do you treasure in your own life that you secretly despise?
—Alexander Payne and Jim Taylor